Walk The Renaissance Walk

A Kid's Guide To Florence, Italy

Photography By John D. Weigand
Poetry By Penelope Dyan

Bellissima Publishing, LLC
Jamul, California
www.bellissimapublishing.com

copyright © 2009 by Penny D. Weigand & John D. Weigand

All rights reserved. No part of this book may be
reproduced or transmitted in any form or by any means,
electronic or mechanical, including photocopying,
recording, or by any other means, or by any information or
storage retrieval system, without permission from the publisher.

ISBN 1-935118-70-6
First Edition

For Paula, a true original

Walk The Renaissance Walk

Bellissima Publishing, LLC

Introduction

Florence, Italy was the home of Dante, who was born in 1267 baptized in its Baptistery. It was also the home of Galileo, Michelangelo, Donatello and many others. It's a fun place for a kid. It is a place that if it is presented correctly can infuse the imagination and enlighten the spirit. Just walking the famous Renaissance Walk will leave you in awe. . . inspired. . . as you realize you are walking where greatness once walked,

Once again Penelope Dyan and John Weigand have joined forces to present another wonderful travel guide for kids, and this one also imparts a very important lesson,

So walk the walk and see the sights, and small the smells of Florence, Italy. Take in its unique beauty. Remember who walked there before you and feel inspired.

Penelope Dyan is an award winning author, poet and illustrator of children's books, and John D. Weigand is a director of television engineering whose photographs can only inspire.

Add this book to your collection of Bellissima Books that are meant for kids, but look great on your coffee table. This book proves once again that Bellissima loves kids, and kids will love this very special Bellissima Book.

Walk The Renaissance Walk

Bellissima Publishing, LLC

Walk The Renaissance Walk

A Kid's Guide To Florence, Italy

Photography By John D. Weigand
Poetry By Penelope Dyan

To get to Florence you can take a train,
After you arrive in Venice by plane.

And then you can walk the Renaissance Walk,
And learn all about the Renaissance as you talk.
Or you can even ride a bike,
If that is what you'd really like,
As through the streets of Florence you will go,
Not to fast and not too slow.
Remembering all all the great men who walked this street,
That now lies beneath your wheels or feet.

You can take a carriage drawn by a horse,
You have this option, always, of course.
As you ride along a Florence street,
Where great men once placed their feet.

You can see the Duomo on the walk,
And you may even stop and gawk,
Because this is something that withstood time,
Something that is quite sublime.

And there is another surprise in store,
As you gaze upon the Baptistery's golden bronze door.

As you travel, block to block,
You see restaurants and shops as you walk.

And here you see hams, and to this I swear,
They're just hanging up there in the air.

A man strums his guitar and makes music sweet,
As he sits and plays beside the street.
As you walk the walk, the 'Renaissance Way,'
You notice it's a lovely day.

The Uffizi Gallery has many statues outside,
And Florence is where once Galileo did reside.
This is his statue that you can see,
Looking as wise as once was he.

And here you see Leonardo Da Vinci stand,
Who dreamed of flying above the land.

You can see the statue of Donatello,
He was a famous artist and quite a fellow.

And here is a statue that holds a surprise. . .

As it comes to life and moves before your eyes.

There is a copy of the David out on the street,
The real Michelangelo statue we have yet to meet.
The original (damaged in 1527) because in a riot broke its arm,
It's inside Galleria dell'Accademia to protect it from harm.

We go to the Old Bridge (Ponte Vecchio) continuing to walk,
And we keep on moving, and we talk.
We wonder if we will run into a ghost,
And if Michelangelo will be our host.
Would he introduce us to the others
Who in their hearts were just like brothers?
Did they live without a care,
As art and scientific thought proliferated everywhere?
And what happened to all the greatness that was once here?
Did it really have to disappear?

And now we feast our hungry eyes,
At the Galleria dell'Accademia, at the artistic and wise.
Yes, this is the place you need to go,
To see the REAL David of Michelangelo.
And perhaps if you look into your very own heart,
You can also create a great work of art.
All you have to do is be one of a kind,
Because an original is so worth the find!

The End
of fakes...the beginning of something real...

www.ingramcontent.com/pod-product-compliance
Ingram Content Group UK Ltd.
Pitfield, Milton Keynes, MK11 3LW, UK
UKHW060137240426
12048UKWH00002B/74